ROLL ON GREAT EARTH

Poems and Illustrations
by
Clare S. Rosenfield

Satya-Light Press
4 Cross Hill Road
Hartsdale, New York 10530

Graphic Design by Marite B. Jones and Shawn Bennett
Technical Assistance by Lindsay Birch

Audio CD version of the poet reading this book
was recorded by Steve Rowland

Website: http://www.contacthealing.com

Email: csr37@columbia.edu

ISBN 0-9726332-0-0

Printed in the United States of America
by Columbia University Printing Services

PERSONAL BLESSING

DEDICATION

To the survival of our Earth and the revival of our humanity
toward one another and all of life
and to the embodiment of that humanity for me from earliest
childhood
my beloved Nanny Fisher
(1883-1970)
May this collection of poems be as a blessing to her and
may her loving soul rest in peace

—

PREFACE

My beloved grandmother, Mamie, used to say, "As if one mother had us all." She was my first contact with a mother earth figure, a nourishing and protective lap/ bosom/ belly/ set of arms. All of the above. She had everything I could dive into and feel safe because of it. She prayed, she blessed, she worried, she loved. She was the first universal-minded person to imprint all of herself onto my child-self. Perhaps that is the origin of my inordinate love for the earth, whom I see as our mother, out of whose body I feel we are all made.

Perhaps that is why I go wild and feel outraged at the slightest hint of racism, religious bias and exclusivity, ethnic hatreds, homophobia, rights violations of all kinds, power inequalities and abuses, excessive nationalism, and specie-ism. Whether such attitudes arise out of ignorance, apathy, or harmful intentions, it seems they all lead to some form of exploitation, torture, and/or killing. Too often the assembly line mentality is transposed to the "industry" of cruelty, ending millions of lives, of both humans and animals, in as streamlined a way as possible, without any tinge of regret, compassion, or regard for the other's independent right to live. We need to call for a halt to this daily horror.

I personally wish that everyone would prioritize the preciousness of each living, breathing life as if each one were one's own.

I want to contribute to that newly awakened consciousness, starting with the discovery of that preciousness in our very own selves. Once life itself is experienced as sacred, then I believe the world could become what it is meant to be–a place in which our children and grandchildren, yours and mine, and each succeeding generation, can safely grow and evolve and blossom fully, can bring forth their purest intentions and manifest their true being.

This set of poems was birthed over a period of twelve years, from the start of the "puzzle" of the Gulf War into the present year when there are more puzzling war whoops in the air. It is my attempt to jolt us from our unconscious resignation and unquestioned acceptance of war and violence as well as from our despair and helplessness. There is "one perfect note" and there is "a chance for peace." Let us sound that note and take that chance.

Clare S. Rosenfield
July 19, 2002

LIST OF POEMS

LIST OF ILLUSTRATIONS

PART ONE
THE PUZZLE OF WAR–PRESENT

Roll On Great Earth

September Eleven

Afghan Desperation

In The Middle

Child Song

Virtual Reality

THE PUZZLE OF WAR

ROLL ON GREAT EARTH

Roll on great earth
borne down upon
yet bearing bearing still
roll on sweet earth
though dirges ring
from west to east
and nothing stops them still
not hearing
still not hearing

What will it take for
them to shake inside
their skins and cease
the fire

Oh dire these times
must we put off till
they put on the skins of
dying men
croaking underneath the
rubble heaped with lifeless then
will they murmur oh what
we have done
what have we
done

SEPTEMBER ELEVEN

A fiendish flare of lightning
a bolt of focused hatred
telescopes birth-years into a blink
discounts the precious the personal
in one hellish maelstrom
robs ravages strikes thousands
of distinct individuals

Where did they go
swirled into the unknown
in so sudden a nightmare
beautiful beings buried in the rubble

Are they halted forever hushed
Where did they go

The space they moved in
did it not part
to honor their passing
grow love like wings
turn hundreds instantly into
persons of valor and magnanimity

Is not that ground
a place of palpable sacredness

Each cherished life
numberless dots of time held
as heart-prints on the soul
each survivor embraced
by global groundswells
grieving for love against all odds

Dignity above onslaught
rises like a lotus out of mud
humaneness of humanity
the ultimate validation

A portal in the human heart opens
impetus for transformation
as harmonies texture us one

AFGHAN DESPERATION

I used to think desperation
belonged to the myopic
stuck in a stance
stubborn in views that
darken the mind like a sunless tent
dwarf tolerance for self and other
I used to believe it was a thing
that could be brushed away like dust
if only the person see straight

until I saw the rock-like faces of Afghan women
lined like cliffs
eaten gaunt by army ants
refugee women and children too
living on a plateau in the middle of no exit
without knowing when the next piece of chapati
will appear in their withered hands
to be chewed and sucked on all day long
to assuage a shrunken stomach
until the next hand-out

I used to think I knew something
until I saw what irreparable damage
has been done to women and children fleeing bombs
eardrums broken
along with hearts
from witnessing one child after another breathe their last
for lack of a mouthful a jacket a tent medicine clean water
for living in unhabitable habitations
from cumulative violations enacted in the name of
in the name of
in the name of

Who will know their names
those whose faces till now have been disallowed
for whom living has been beyond desperate
who somehow still endure
for how many more belabored breaths
frostbitten footsteps
inedible mouthfuls
for how many more days and nights of desperation

IN THE MIDDLE

IN THE MIDDLE

Her child runs to her bedside
"Mommy, I'm burning!"
Her body has caught fire.
It is the middle of the night
the middle of a nightmare
the middle of cluster bombs
landed in the middle of families
innocent Afghan families
sleeping in their beds one minute
awakened to horror the next

She smothers the burning flesh of her child
with a ragged piece of blanket
carries her enfolded in her arms
rushes to the hospital
hours of anxiety
a lifetime of scars begun

The beginning of her voice
"Why do you drop such things where people live?
These are meant for tanks
not people
Look at my weeping child
see our people's pain
where my heart used to be
a huge cavern of sorrow

"Look! over there–huge trees gone--burned to the ground
our orchards destroyed
Money promised
for rebuilding our lives
where is it?
No one to turn to--
educate my children–how?
Warlords vying again
You have rid us of the Taliban
but what of the devastation you have wrought?"

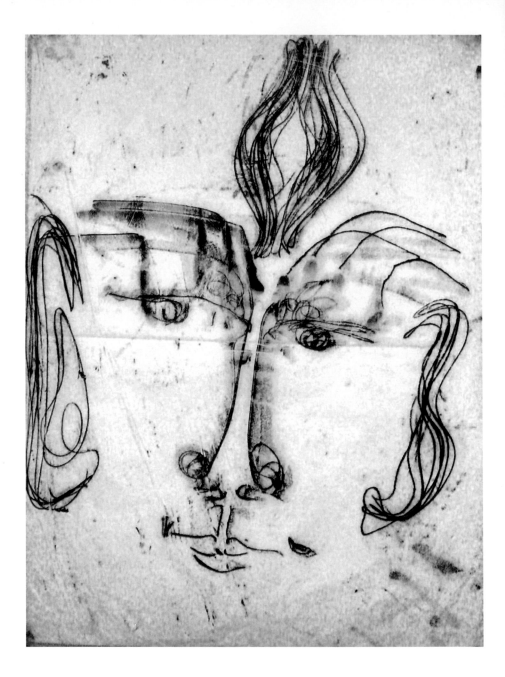

MY BROTHER GOD <u>ME</u> GAVE

CHILD SONG

I'm wise beyond my years,
they say
wise beyond my tears.
When trees bend down to kiss my curls
I wish that all the little girls
could be so touched as I

I soar beyond the sky
they say
beyond the cotton pie
When on my shoulders birds alight
I fly beyond the darkest night
and float for hours on high

I see beyond the face
they say
They call it inner grace
When men with smiling faces wave
their plans to draft him to the grave
I pull him far away
My brother God <u>me</u> gave

I speak my mind and heart
they say
I haven't any art
It's just my way to shout and scream
why should I give my cherished dream
for feet to trample on?
It must live on and on

I am a child of God
they say
I say you too are God
They scratch their facts and numbers down
upon the sands of time to drown
and miss the ocean roar
That's what <u>I</u> came here for

VIRTUAL REALITY

At first seems solid
substantial
persons things places
in truth a vast array of whirling energies
thought forms meeting thought forms
in multiples
join categories
gather momentum
form shadows
subterranean sub-conscious
swim with fish
feed on unheard shrieks
casks of grief tightly shut
grudge-formations
dream-drops
underwater for eons
collide with zillions of particles
create conflict
build mutual hatreds
or mutual agreements
color auras
impact atmosphere
the degree of light or darkness
of our sliver of life
as piece by piece
intention by intention
vibration by vibration
it enters in
to the kaleidoscope
and every less than the blink of an eye
transforms our world

PART TWO
THE PUZZLE OF WAR–PAST

The Puzzle Of War

For My Beloved Dad

No Man's Land

A Dot In Time

Upon Seeing The Ashes Of Gandhi

Arise

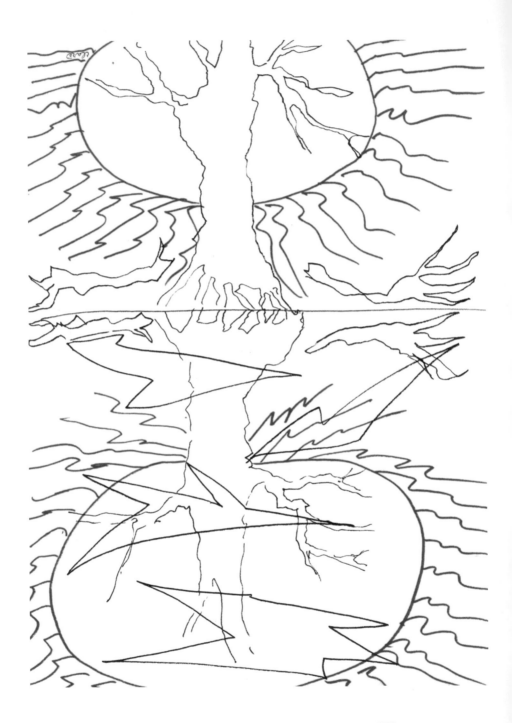

HIGH NOON AND ONE MORE CRACK

12

THE PUZZLE OF WAR

A tree outlined thinly
on thin ice
like dead branches
about to move
into dissolution

High noon
and one more crack
gone from our sight
men who
one minute ago
breathed
inside their installation
blasted
from their spot
precisely
into myriad pieces

The puzzle of war
where the whole
can never equal
the devastation
wrought by its parts
sense gone berserk
which yesterday reasoned
it was better
to sell to one's enemies
than to shoot them
outright

FOR MY BELOVED DAD OF BLESSED MEMORY

What for? What for? you cried
people killing each other
what for?
I too ask this
anguished already twice in the space of sixty days
by the loss of two dear to me
so dear
you and he

And now I angst for souls unknown
far off across the planet
hovering round the cradle of civilization
Mesopotamia of the Tigris
Babylon of the Euphrates
my third grade geography lesson leaping
from the pages
my heart too
longs for sensibleness
struggles against despair
just sinks below the horizon like the sun
to nestle invisible
beneath the sea

My peace indwells the waters of my soul
renders me oceanic
a space to hold
each piece of the kaleidoscopic drama
tanks creeping
war-whoops swelling
death throes moaning
gas masks stalking
faces distorted by the call
of duty unprotested

My peace is witness
stands firm apart
as decisions on the march daily defy reason

My peace speaks steady
wordless
for life yet to be lived

for breaths yet to be inhaled
for humans yet to be evolved
for a planet yet to survive

My only consolation
that you
my beloved Dad
and Daniel
my dear friend
have been spared
this freshest pain

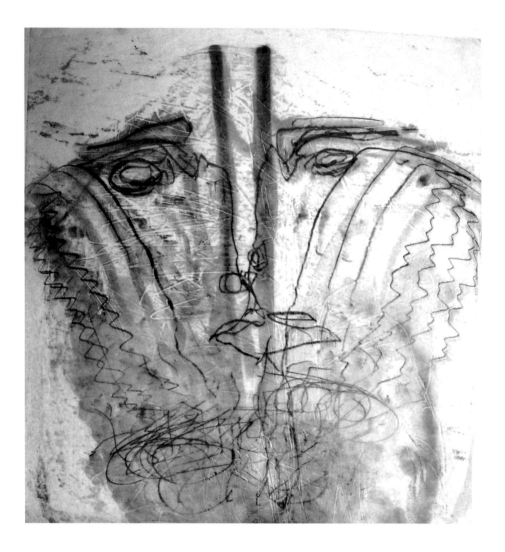

NO MAN'S LAND

NO MAN'S LAND

Hungry eyes look up
the same sun there
I see here

Frightened child-eyes
grip a skyscape
streaked with flashing
thunderous in implication

Sun cannot protect now
though it rises and sets
with accuracy

Homedwellers made nomads now
in no man's land
the legacy of minds gone crazed
with oil
and my way's gotta be
the best
the winner
eyes that know to count
but not to see
life

Screams wail on
deaf ears only

Men with power get
gnawed like a rat
shrink
unnoticed
into a tiny fist
then an empty pod
next
try to open
their mouths
barely a whisper emerges
then a rattle
nothing more

A DOT IN TIME

Rosary fingers turn
trench-dwellers eye empty bags
fear lurks
larger than the dunes
endlessly grown into
disappeared edges
dropped into
horizon pits

The mirage of peace
quenches
no questions
disallowed by the sure
doubters trammeled
by the beat of deadly drums
hollow now for good
the last vestiges of tears
scraped dry

Heartbeats soften no longer
a lost land
a wasteland these
and the cycle of the ages
keeps turning the pages
backward
till belief and doubt
braggart and coward
victor and loser
are but
a dot in time

And the desert looms supreme
engulfs the gulf
between the poles
whose minds refuse to meet
in common humanity
and so
do so
inside the common sand

UPON SEEING THE ASHES OF GANDHI

Strewn into the sea
lifetime shrunk into handful
time evaporates
our battle cries
soundless whimpers
useless
useless
better to toss them overboard
before one has but ashes in hand
fiery forays of illusory logic
better to silence them
before they destroy us all

Could we simply sit
round the world
in circles
hand in hand
drown
in one another's eyes
and birth our universe anew

Could we stop stoking memory's furnace
with withered skins of past loves
turned hateful
of old grudges rekindled

Could we just sit around the fountain
in silent wonder
planless
a course with no requirements
except
to audit well
the sound of one's being
being
the sound of one Being
being

ARISE

Arise oh hearts of valor
rouse yourselves
not to the whine
and whinny of small men
in helmets and guns dressed
to the kill
nor rise to the patter
of the prattling patriot
nor mire down
in mind trenches

Drench instead
in love potions
that draw you out
from your teacup
into space-embrace

Nectarous in omni-vision
go the living
daily forth

PART THREE
ONE PERFECT NOTE

21

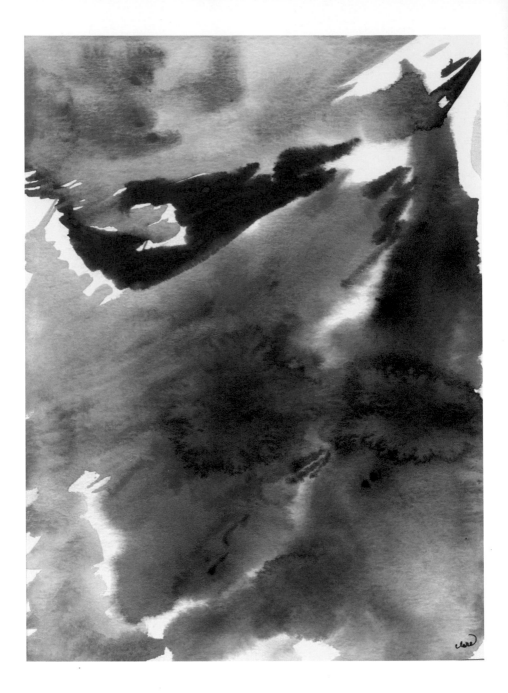

FULL FRAGRANCE

ONE PERFECT NOTE

"There is one perfect note," she said,
the goddess said to me,
"and she who tunes to that," said she,
"tunes to the harmony."

"Yes, she who tunes to that," she said,
"moves with eternity,
"rests in her peace, lays down her head,
"and rests her soul in me."

"What note is that, oh friend?" I asked,
"what perfect note is that?"
"It's called the harmlessness," she said,
"it's that and all is that."

"It's the perfection of thy soul,
"it's thee intrinsically,
"it draws full fragrance from thy heart,
"gives forth so easefully."

I tuned to harmlessness, it's true,
and found my unity,
just tuned to love for life, that's all,
and let myself be free.

STILL A JUNGLE

A jungle this world
green life sings out
every where

as it was

before it was cut apart
paved
jumbled
combined
exhumed
built upon

as it is truly

still a jungle
still utters sounds by night
by day
one huge jungle
of creatures
ever in bloom
and so are we

Civilized is one
who lives among the living
and does not pounce

Civilized is one
who extols this jungle
gives green its due
and life its honor
equally sees eye to eye

Civilized is one
who wants no more
than what
out of creative bounty
mother nature provides
who lives a simple life
unencumbered
free

EPITAPH

Below a mourning mother earth man lies
though flailing out once more can hold no thing
What kind of peace can he to mind now bring--
atrocities he lived--in grief he dies

To visions of a better world he flies
but colored scarlet red his memories sting
He's now a beggar whom he once thought king--
what heart of mercy dares to hear his cries

It will be his own which hears his own--
throbbing he will feel the pain he's given
to innocents whose skin and sinew ate

oblivious to shriek and squeal or moan
of parent or of child to gallows driven
as empty words of peace fell in his plate

SPIRIT DIALOGUE

AN UNUSUAL MEETING

As I hurry towards my hut in the woods
a loud thumping sends tremors
through my legs
Safety awaits me there
a warm vigorous fire
fresh pea soup steaming hot
but I cannot proceed
have to whirl round and face
those sounds
Who could it be--
a huge creature reclaiming his territory?
a trespasser?
someone who wants to attack me?

I stop and turn
The path is empty
Who's there--
come on out
I could be your friend

No answer--
emptiness where I supposed a massive solid something
no more deafening thuds
Bewildered
might as well start off again
but no sooner than I do
noise thunders after me
I halt
All right
are you out there or pounding in my own brain?
Who are you-- what are you--
do you have something to tell me?
I'll listen
I promise

Silence
then a voice
I am not here but I am
I am under the earth
and on top
I am in your mind

and out of it
I am the sounds of agony and pain
of beings crying out
for solace and for rest
from the cruelties of mankind
I am the repository of all grief all sorrow
Hear me
if you can be my friend
and look me in the eyes
Though I am invisible I am not unreal--
See me in your heart
see me in the depths of others

I gasp not knowing what to say--
silence then a whisper
Why me-- why talk to me?

Because you have not been willing
to see me before
You've been ignoring me
I nod humbled

But I am not blaming you
Please do not feel crushed
I'm calling on you
I need help--
will you help me?

Oh yes-- how can I--
what can I do?

Take me in your arms-- my friend
just hold me–would you please?

I open my arms
feel the roar of grief
and pounding heart of pain
come into my embrace
accepted accepted
I hold him gently lovingly
We sob together a long long time
then he is gone

CHILDREN

Children the children
answers wrapped within
each a precious diamond-bearer

Open your eyes
oh grown-over ones
see their radiance wisdom realness
how it refuses to be choked
or trampled

Let them speak
listen
to the truth on their lips
mirror them
so they can tune
to their own silent vibrancy
and glimpse the eye
at its source
as it gazes undiverted
upon the point
omniversal cradles them in

each one of them held
each one of us
held

VALENTINE'S DAY IN THE CITY

I rush past cement and glass
huge vertical monoliths
shoulders square and erect
the pride of Manhattan
my coat held close against greyness
a chill that hangs like gauze
till I chance upon a direct line from the east
some folds of sun-cloth
to wrap round my uplifted face
imagine this city without concrete
sun's hems would caress my cheeks
all day long

My steps pick up and halt
this time for a man seated flat
so low on the hard cold pavement
I don't see how
until I gasp
He has no legs
When I bend to hand him my dollar
I meet his doe eyes
and a wooden peg for a finger
am stupefied he has no wheelchair
No services for the disabled?
How does he survive?
Where to pee?
Does someone drop him off ?
exploit him for cash?
Was he a land mine victim?
Why did I not ask him all this?
Too repulsed to look for long
at his uncomplaining face?

I hurry on to catch my train
pass a man madly ringing a bell
Happy Valentine's Day folks
smile and say I love you to someone
No one looks at him
I berate myself for not taking the day
to find help for the legless man

Someone must provide for him
I rationalize or he would not be there

And of course
I have things to do
things to do
What *thing* is more important?

All this mental turmoil
while heart sits sad and stirred
sends him healing
wants a better life for him
for all in need real need
and this is real need
I remember this world is not perfect
nor am I
make space to co-exist with persons
and sufferings
just be with them
just be with them

LET NATURE FILL OUR CUP

BLOODLESS

So long as mother earth is offered blood
instead of tears of sorrow for the pain
that men of "peace" do wreak on her again
by daily spitting bones upon her mud

So long as babes as innocent as Christ
all creatures God-endowed upon this earth
are promised certain death right from their birth
fated to be hooked or clubbed or sliced

So long our work for war-less life's a waste
for tongues which chew on victims call in vain
for men to halt a race all deem insane
while tyrannized by such a thing as taste

Let nature fill our cup with fruit and grain
and fashion minds to bloodlessness again

TALE OF THE TURKEY

Once upon a time
there was a turkey telling time--
he didn't tell it just the way that you and I do tell
he told it like the prophets do of heaven and of hell

He said it's time you human folk start listening to me
I represent tomorrows when thanksgivings won't be free
Thanksgiving's time for killing
has just seen the last of day
'cause hell's in store for gobblers
who give thanks while gobbling me

Thanks and killing hand in hand have had it damned kaput
no time for socializing while you suck my juicy foot
'cause the day of reckoning's coming
and you reckoned wrong I reckon
Do you see those writings beckon
you to face your past and all

Can you do it –can you face it
can you stand up bright and tall
to the history before you where such deadly deeds are written
how can you erase what's there

Well I'll tell you how dear gobbler--it's by stopping time right now
and by taking time to vow
that right now and hence forever
never more to eat the kill
that some poor soul had to bludgeon
with his knife or hammer drill

Then I'll reckon you can reckon on a respite on your time
and instead of dying sooner and of living as if dead
you can give your hearts for living
and can dance the song of creatures
who in being spared their life
will give thanks to you their helper
and protect you their protector
and thanksgiving day will have its day
the whole your lifetime long

34

PART FOUR
A CHANCE FOR PEACE

A CHANCE FOR PEACE

A CHANCE FOR PEACE

In a pause between breaths
a chance for peace
Track that moment
and there is landing

I invite myself
into its under-belly
dwell in a ground
below which I cannot fall
moist with kisses
no lips could ever reach

Here
I could stay
the only place
I can call my own

As worlds whirl
out of control
glare
throw daggers
retaliate
as mouths spew hatred
fuel fury

what would happen
if haters stopped
if blamers ceased
if all eyes softened
chose to be silent
for a moment

let out a sigh
and dropped into the pause
between breaths
touched the under-belly of heart-space
opened to the peace goddess
who has been waiting
since the big bang
for just one instant
of recognition

AMONG THE BARK-FOLK

HEART-CONNECTIONS

Sisterly
I walk among the bark-folk
disrobed by winter
heavy with snow-child
I ache for their forbearance
as stolidly they await a springtime air
and wonder

What kind of power do I have
barely a slender reed
a wisp of a leaf
I am
the better to feel the wind
I say
whistle through my ears
tousle my brows
invite me to sup upon stars
while to earth
I have tenuous links
by just the soles
of my feet

Am I as helpless as masses
who huddle in world creeping famine
while men of little brain plot
to fight enemies
as yet unseen in themselves
What weight is this
in the cavernous inner lining
of my heart
longing to forge connections
with that place in each human
which by just a drop
from head into heart
could disarm enmities in seconds
and sprout anew
a healing hopeful springtime

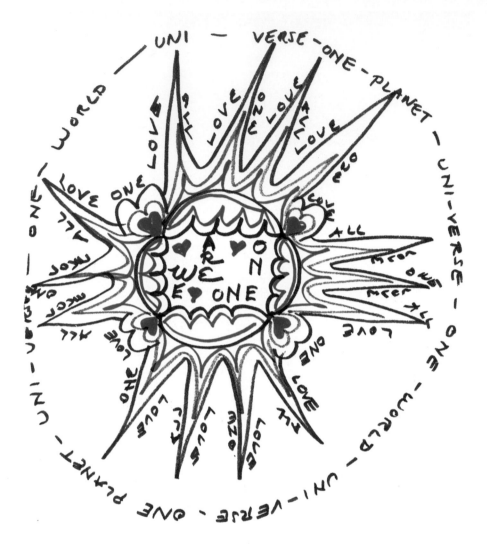

ONE WORLD ONE UNIVERSE

A PLEDGE

I pledge allegiance
to the universe of all life
and to the reality
for which it stands
one family
indivisible
with liberty
and equality
for all

IN MERCIFUL ABIDES

MERCY

Children are just growing babes
their shoots are soft and tender
have mercy mothers mercy
be careful how you tend them

Some folks have bellies gaping wide
wounded from no supper
have mercy men of armaments
stop feeding full your pride

Of all who share this plot of earth
the creatures are squeezed out
en-caged conveyor belted killed
have mercy mankind mercy

We starry-eyed with innocence
ignore our other side
at times abuser and abused
have mercy lovers mercy

Some fellows have no chance and yet
the sun shines equally
on those who blame and those who move
into the possible

Have mercy on each living thing
have mercy on your lives
tend to the garden of your heart
and co-create your world

Have mercy on your ignorance
which made you merciless
sing praises to your wakening
live peaceable your spirit

As softening your heart grows real
in gentleness births spring
abides in readiness abides
in merciful abides

FROM THE COSMIC DEEP

UNSEEN HELPERS

Great stalks of wheat are swaying
take a bow
as wind takes turns
with smiling sun and rain
and children tanned a toasty golden brown
run hungrily to plates of hearty grain

Elsewhere on pavement
miles of arid shops
where cash is poured as freely
as the sweat
which poor men give in toil
that hardly stops
though for it there is nothing they
can get

Sunken eyes aglow
with burning heat
are not aware how long
this drought will last
mothers' breasts gone dry
feel but defeat
in vain try searching
for some crumbs repast

More is less
and less is more
they say

Could those of us who see this
truly live
in such a way that
all we do
is give
then surely unseen helpers from
the cosmic deep
would come and multiply our blessings manifold
and help us
tend the starving
poor and old

45

INHALE THE JUICY TANGERINES AND SCARLETS

THE ALCHEMY OF INNOCENCE

Inhale the juicy
tangerines and scarlets
golden-oranges and yellowy-limes
as they creep up
leafy veins transforming

Distill each pristine color
into the well of your earnest intentions

After all
without guile they exist
as pure power
like guardian angels in clusters
like siblings of
peony petals and forsythia bushes
hydrangea blossoms and grape vines
pomegranate seeds and fields of grain
like all that has been fruitful and multiplied

Could we absorb deep their sap of innocence
pour it into our own
that we lovers of our earth
and the alchemy of blossoming
may prevail
steadfast bear witness
to the splendor
of consciousness
not gone awry

A SPIDER

A spider climbed up and down
what he thought to be
a massive series of mountains.
I told him, "No,
that cannot be.
Those verticals steeped in green
and spread beneath my feet,
mountains they are not."

He merely shook his head,
sucked in his spittle
and carried on his valiant way.

But when I closed my eyes that night,
I saw he'd flashed
before my inner vision
this:

"The world is not centered
in you!"

PLENTIFUL

In land of plentiful
abide
we pile the plates
as high the greeds exceed
the needs can hardly
keep up sums
increase
till matter-heavy
the scale tips
and at the other end
are endings
agonizing
for the helpless
are we?

Helpless?

Buried in plenty
numbness
or inertia?

Can we
tip the balance back
grant that it be
more blessed to
give
than any other thing
cannot take with you
daily sharing
of the heart in open
sprouting
can

ONE MOTHER OF US ALL

ONE MOTHER OF US ALL

Mother mother
earthmother
earthmother
groundmother
mother ground
groundmother
brown mother
ground mother
brown ground
motherground
mother mother
brown earth
brown trees
treemother
trees' mother
mother tree
mother mother
bush mother
mother mother
buds' mother
bush buds
budding green
mother budding
early spring
spring buds
mother's buds
mother's mother's buds
mother's mother's mother's buds

one mother your mother
one mother my mother
mother mother their mother
mother mother our mother
holy mother
ground mother
round mother my mother
motherground our mother
all mothers our mother
one mother of us all
we

OTHER BOOKS BY CLARE S. ROSENFIELD

Ten Lives of the Buddha: Siamese Temple Paintings and Jataka Tales
by Elizabeth Wray, Clare Rosenfield, and Dorothy Bailey

Dance Upon The Winds Swept Cloudless

Seasonals

A Man With A Vision

Reverence for All Life and Vegetarianism
by Clare Rosenfield and Linda Segall

To Light One Candle: Universal Prayers for Peace
by Clare Rosenfield and Pramoda Chitrabhanu

CLARE S. ROSENFIELD

Clare S. Rosenfield, also known as Satya (meaning essence or truth), is a writer, meditation teacher, healer, and social worker who has founded a holistic approach to self-healing called Contact Healing™.

A Smith College graduate and former French teacher in Boston, Lagos, and Bangkok, Clare received both her M.A. in French and later an M.S. degree in Social Work from Columbia University.

Drawing upon more than thirty years of experience integrating therapeutic approaches from East and West, she empowers people with self-healing meditations, breathing experiments, inner journeys, and the cultivation of compassion toward oneself and all of life. Through her work with the Global Healing Foundation as well as through her seminars, writings, and one-to-one healing sessions, she inspires people to uncover their personal truth, to cherish life, and to care deeply for our earth.

Clare lives in New York with her husband, Dr. Allan Rosenfield, who is Dean of the Mailman School of Public Health of Columbia University. They have two adult children, a two and a half year old granddaughter and a newborn grandson. To invite Clare for poetry readings or Contact Healing ™ seminars, to schedule individual sessions, or to place orders for this book and/or for reproductions of the illustrations:
e-mail csr37@columbia.edu or visit http://www.contacthealing.com.

REPRODUCTIONS OF THE POET'S ILLUSTRATIONS
ARE AVAILABLE AT WWW.CONTACTHEALING.COM

"Roll On Great Earth"
front & back cover

15"x20.5"

Touch drawing

"Personal Blessing"

20.5"x15"

Touch drawing

"The Puzzle of War"

20.5"x15"

Touch drawing

"In the Middle"

20.5"x15"

Touch drawing

"My Brother God <u>Me</u> Gave"

20.5"x15"

Touch drawing

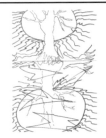

"High Noon and One More Cracl"

12"x8.5"

Pen and ink drawing

"No Man's Land"

20.5"x15"

Touch drawing

"Full Fragrance"

12"x9"

Watercolor

"Spirit Dialogue"

20.5"x15"

Touch drawing

"Let Nature Fill Our Cup"

12"x9"

Watercolor

" A Chance for Peace"

12"x9"

Pen and ink drawing

"Among the Bark-Folk"

Acrylic painting

"One World One Universe"

12"x9"

Pen and ink drawing

"In Merciful Abides"

12"x9"

Watercolor

"From the Cosmic Deep"

22"x12.5"

Pastel

"Inhale The Juicy Tangerines And Scarlets"

20"x15"

Acrylic painting

"One Mother of Us All"

15"x20"

Acrylic painting

www.contacthealing.com